How to harness the value of Bitcoin without having to sell it

Juraj Bednár

© 2024 Juraj Bednár
For informational and technical purposes only, always consult tax advisors, legal counsel and up to date technical information

Video course and up to date information

This book cannot be always up to date and it can't contain video content, although I tried to include as many screenshots as I found useful for demonstrating these concept. If you want, you can upgrade to an online course. You can find it at my website hackyourself.io/shop and use a coupon **HARNESSBOOK** to get a discount.

Table of contents

INTRODUCTION	6
WHY DON'T RICH PEOPLE SELL THEIR ASSETS?	7
THE PRINCIPLE OF COLLATERALISED LENDING	9
EXAMPLE OF A LOAN THROUGH MAKERDAO (OASIS BORROW)	19
AAVE PLATFORM ON THE AVALANCHE NETWORK	24
USING THE NATIVE AVAX BITCOIN BRIDGE	33
MORE EFFICIENT POSITION OPENING WITH RESPECT TO FEES	43

SPARK.FI – AAVE-LIKE EXPERIENCE WITH MORE STABLE INTEREST RATES	45
FIREFISH PLATFORM	47
BITCOIN FUTURES	60
FUTURES USING 10101 APP	66
WHEN TO REPAY THE LOAN?	75
RISKS AND HOW TO DEAL WITH THEM	77
HOW TO USE THE LOAN	87
CONCLUSION	89
BONUS: THE OTHER SIDE OF THE LOAN - INVESTING AND EARNING FIAT INTEREST	90

Introduction

Even the most hard-core Bitcoin HODLers sometimes must pay rent, mortgage, utility bill or school tuition for their kids. Selling Bitcoins not only comes with negative emotions of parting with your precious satoshis, but often other inconveniences such as taxes and tax declarations that make the situation even worse. I can't help you with Bitcoin taxation, there are other experts for that, but what if we could find a way to pay the rent, the mortgage, the electricity, the hardware wallet, and the kids' school without having to sell the Bitcoin in the first place? We could avoid a potentially taxable event altogether. Please note though, that I **do not know the laws of country where you have potential tax obligations**. This is a technological overview of lending options, not tax advice. For tax advice, seek a licensed professional.

Also please note, that most of the projects I talk about explicitly forbid use by citizens or residents of United States of America. Sorry, dear yankees, we love you, but your government makes it so hard to create compliant services, that most projects and companies just exclude you and serve customers that live somewhere else.

Why don't rich people sell their assets?

Let us first examine how it is possible that rich people do not pay (a lot of) taxes. Elon Musk, Jeff Bezos and others have, of course, enough money to pay the best accountants and the best tax-optimization schemes that work and allow them not to pay taxes and at the same time not end up with a fine or jail time. Their companies often use these tax schemes, but we are talking about individuals now.

The reality is often surprisingly simple - those who do not earn an income do not have to pay income taxes. Those who do not realize capital gains do not pay capital gains tax. A common way billionaires finance their lifestyle is by borrowing. They go to a private bank and say "I own shares in my company and would like to use them as a collateral and take out a loan". Of course, if they give the bank $10 million worth of stock, they can borrow a lower value - say $1 million or $5 million (this ratio is called LTV - loan to value and it protects the lender against sudden drops of the collateral's value).

The advantage of this approach is not only tax-related, but the shares that are pledged to the bank as a collateral allow the owner to keep the stock's voting rights, for example, so they don't lose control of their company. If the value of the shares plummets, the bank can call on the borrower to repay the loan or replenish the collateral. If the owner fails to do so, the bank will sell the shares on an open market (this is in many countries a taxable event for the shareholder if the sale occurs at a price higher than the purchase price).

Can we take a similar approach in the cryptocurrency environment? Thanks to the emerging DeFi (decentralized finance) environment, it is possible. Bitcoin maximalists may have an unpleasant aftertaste when reading these words, but I remind you of your alternative - sell your Bitcoins and maybe even pay a tax. So, let's look at the first option - DeFi.

The principle of collateralised lending

Collateralised lending works the same way as it does for billionaires with their stock. Collateral can be anything the platform supports - and most platforms support most coins that have good liquidity and a well-defined market price. Bitcoin, for example.

The process is very similar regardless of the platform - you put up the collateral, look at the terms, choose what you want to borrow, and then sell what you borrowed on the market. After that, some care or "babysitting" is required - monitoring the interest rates and whether there is a risk of liquidation (in case the value of collateral goes close to the value that could trigger the liquidation event).

Depositing collateral and selecting the parameters

The form of the collateral may vary. In some protocols, you can even combine it - for example, on the Aave platform, you can use both Bitcoin and Ethereum as collateral at the same time. The value of the collateral adds up.

Where do you put it? For centralised platforms, you deposit the collateral directly into the Bitcoin wallet to which the platform holds the keys. That means you lose ownership of the keys, but the legal fiction of ownership remains with you, so in most countries, this is not a taxable event (but as with all tax and accounting issues – please consult a licensed professional). Personally, I don't trust these third parties enough - not only they might not protect my Bitcoins sufficiently, but more importantly, they can't protect my personal data, which they unfortunately collect.

The other option is to get on a smart contract platform like Ethereum, various Layer Two protocols of Ethereum (Optimism, Polygon, Arbitrum), Avalanche or Solana (I have no experience with Solana so far and I do not recommend it for new users). The protocols there are largely decentralized, open, and have undergone some non-trivial test of time.

Personally, I would use the platforms that have been around the longest such as Aave, Compound or MakerDAO. Collateral ownership in such a case is no longer protected by your private keys alone, but by a smart contract algorithm that defines the terms of collateral withdrawal. These are in practice user-friendly - all the protocols mentioned above allow you to withdraw any excess collateral. That might be useful for example if the value of your collateral goes up and you do not need that much collateral to cover the loan. If you repay the loan with interest, you can withdraw all of the collateral. If the value of the collateral falls below a predetermined multiple of the amount owed (which includes outstanding interest), the system will trigger an auction of your collateral, thus paying off the amount owed.

What happens to the collateral in normal situations varies from protocol to protocol. In the case of MakerDAO, the collateral just sits in the smart contract account. In the case of the Aave protocol, the collateral is added by the protocol to the pool of money to lend, and so "your" coins are lent out in the market at market interest (which is determined by the ratio of the demand for loans versus the amount of funds deposited). This has both advantages and disadvantages.

The advantage of MakerDAO (as opposed to Aave) is that fewer things can go wrong. Of course, an unexpected market situation can cause maximum liquidation by auction, but you can't have a situation where collateral is not returned because someone else has borrowed it and not paid it back. On the other hand, in Aave's case, you are earning interest on the collateral. And because the loan is over-collateralized, you are earning interest on a higher value than you are borrowing (because you borrowed at most half, probably even a third of the value you deposited as collateral). That does not necessarily mean that you are paid for taking a loan, the interest rates on collateral can be 0.1% p.a., while the interest you pay on the loan can be 2.5% p.a. for example.

The interest effect of collateral can be significantly higher than the interest on the loan though. Let's assume for simplicity that we deposit 1 BTC (in the form of WBTC on MakerDAO or in the form of WBTC.e on Aave on the Avalanche network) and we want to borrow a dollar stablecoin worth 0.33 BTC (according to the current exchange rate, which is not important now).

At the time of writing, the WBTC-C vault on MakerDAO requires an interest rate payment (called a "stability fee" in Maker DAO) of 1.5% p.a. You must have a WBTC value greater than 175% of the amount borrowed for the position not to be liquidated.

If we borrow through Aave, the interest on the loan might be higher than 1.5% p.a., but the platform pays us interest on the collateral (and it's good to have collateral at least 3 times the loan amount in most cases). This should be taken into account, because often a loan through a money market platform can be more profitable, even though the interest on the loan itself may be higher at a first glance.

A collateral that is different than WBTC can also earn you significantly higher interest, but here the question is what you want to HODL. As for the loan, it's important to understand not only what the interest rate is (these vary for different stablecoins), but also that what you borrow, you will have to pay back. In case you want to gamble, if you believe that a stablecoin will lose value, it might be a good idea to borrow that one because you can buy it cheaper and get out of the loan more cheaply if you are right. In the past, such a problem happened, for example, with the MIM (Magic Internet Money) stablecoin of the Abracadabra.money project, when it traded for $0.92. Beware, stablecoin can trade for more than a dollar if people need it to pay off a loan, for example in times of rising interest rates.

The platform you want to use should be chosen not only on the basis of interest rates, but also on the basis of fees, including fees for future transactions - possible replenishment of collateral, partial repayment of the loan, withdrawal of excess collateral, and so on. That's why I personally prefer either layer two protocols on Ethereum or the Avalanche network, which has slightly more predictable fees than the Ethereum network itself. Avalanche C-Chain is an EVM (Ethereum Virtual Machine) compatible network and runs the same time-tested DeFi protocols as you know on Ethereum. Of course, use platforms that you trust and know how to use.

How to get collateral on the target platform

If you insist on having the collateral in Bitcoin, you need to somehow change the form of Bitcoin from BTC on the Bitcoin network (whether onchain or lightning) to wrapped Bitcoin (WBTC on the Ethereum network or WBTC.e on the Avalanche network). The provider of this token is a third party, so it does not have the same security as Bitcoin, for which you directly own the private keys. I can't say whether the providers of this token can be trusted, but the fact is that enough users trust it. According to statistics as of March 14, 2022, there are 85 times more Bitcoins locked up in WBTC than in the Lightning network and the Liquid sidechain (Lightning public channels and Liquid similarly have about 3500 BTC). Of course, there are many private channels in the Lightning network, so we can't say for sure how many Bitcoins are in it, but what is certain is that locking Bitcoin value into WBTC comes as a good idea to at least an order of magnitude more Bitcoin hodlers at the moment than using Lightning. Of course, an order of magnitude more users could be wrong, too.

A direct "wrapping process" is not publicly available, so you need to reach for a decentralized or at least non-KYC exchange, such as sideshift.ai (unfortunately the Invity metasearch engine does not support wbtc). The other option is to get the token of the target network (eth or avax) or some token on the target network and use a decentralized exchange like ParaSwap, UniSwap, etc. Here again, watch out for taxable events - "wrapping" Bitcoin should not be a taxable event because you are not selling or buying any Bitcoin, but changing Bitcoin to Ethereum may already be a taxable event - although depending on your tax domicile, you may be able to account for the purchase and subsequent immediate sale as a tax neutral transaction - check with your accountant in the country where you are a tax resident. This text does not give tax or accounting advice.

You also should buy an Ethereum or Avax token (depending on the platform you're using) so you have a way to pay the fees.

Choosing a stablecoin to borrow from the platform

Once you have chosen your platform, terms and conditions and deposited your collateral, you can choose the stablecoin you wish to borrow. After you borrow it, you can then sell it on the market (immediate sale does not usually trigger a taxable event, because the exchange rate between the time you borrowed it and the time you sold it did not change).

Always consider that what you are borrowing is what you have to return in the future. If you post collateral in the form of WBTC and borrow Ethereum, you have effectively opened a short position on Ethereum against WBTC. If Ethereum rises in value, you will have to return the same amount of ETH that you borrowed, plus interest! Therefore, in almost any case, it is not wise to borrow cryptocurrencies unless you want to short them (which I don't recommend).

Stablecoin can then be converted through non-KYC exchanges into something you can sell on the market. For example, you can exchange them for Monero, Ethereum, or sell the stablecoin directly. Beware, if you exchange them for Bitcoin (which is the easiest to sell) and you also own Bitcoins (such as the ones you put on collateral), there may still be a taxable event. That's why it's a good idea to sell something you don't otherwise own and exchange it at the time of sale for the fiat you want to get in the end. For example, if you don't own Monero and you find a buyer for Monero, then if you quickly exchange the borrowed stablecoin for Monero and exchange it for fiat, there will be no exchange rate change that could cause a tax event.

Example of a loan through MakerDAO (Oasis Borrow)

We are going to use Oasis Borrow to borrow DAI stablecoin pegged to USD. Please note that MakerDAO introduced minimal amounts for borrowing, they are different for each "vault" (i.e. combination of backing, LTV and interest rate), but if you want to just try it out, MakerDAO platform will probably not be the best place to start unless you want to borrow 5000-7500 DAI to start. If you want to try this collateralized loan with lower amounts, see next chapters for examples using different platforms. I wanted to start with this project because it is the oldest and it is very simple to setup.

The first step is to install an extension such as Metamask or Frame.sh and **link it to your hardware wallet**. Follow the documentation and be sure to use the hardware wallet. Both extensions can use a hardware wallet. Their function is to turn your "normal" browser such as Firefox or Chrome into a "web3 browser" that can interact with web3 applications. If your web3 browser works and is set-up, you can go to Oasis.app, which is the official MakerDAO Project (DAI) lending interface.

In the top menu, select Borrow, choose the collateral type (in our case BTC) and choose one of the options for loan parameters and collateral forms (WBTC's competitor is RENBTC). We can see that different so-called "vaults" have different borrowing parameters. For example, WBTC-C currently has an interest rate of only 0.75% p.a., but at a collateral value of 175% of the loan value, it will already liquidate the position (so it is a good idea to hold WBTC at least three times the amount we want to borrow). WBTC-A has a higher interest, but it is liquidated only when the value drops to 145% of the loan value. Not all vaults need to be available, some have already reached their capacity.

In our case we choose WBTC-C.

At this stage, you will need to connect a wallet (by selecting from supported wallets, such as Metamask, Frame or a wallet that supports the WalletConnect protocol). Once connected, a message will be displayed:

Welcome

It looks like you're new to Oasis.app or are using a new device to connect. For added security, please sign a message with your wallet to continue.

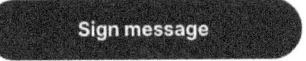

Sign message

Disconnect

This message says that we need to use the wallet key to sign the message. We will need to confirm this on the hardware wallet. (You're using a hardware wallet, right? Right???). We'll confirm the terms of service.

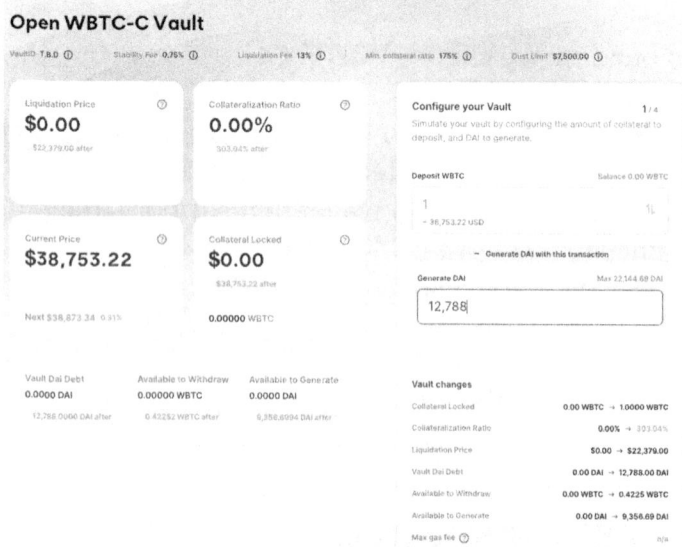

In the last window we will open the parameters where we set how much WBTC we want to insert (I used 1 WBTC from the example above), how much DAI we want to generate (before typing the value we need to click on Generate DAI so the input box where we type the amount appears).

In this case, I put 12788 DAI (so $12788), which is about a third of the collateral value. On the right, we can see the changes that occur when the next couple of transactions are confirmed.

The locked collateral changes from 0 WBTC to 1 WBTC. The collateral to loan ratio will be 302.04%. The liquidation rate is $22379 - so if the Bitcoin rate falls to $22379, our collateral will go to auction (and we will pay a penalty, at the time of writing it is 12.5%). We will owe 12788 DAI. If the exchange rate doesn't change, we can theoretically pull up to 0.4225 WBTC of excess collateral, but this will increase our risk of liquidation for any small downward movement in the Bitcoin exchange rate. We can also borrow an extra 9356.69 DAI, but again we increase the risk of liquidation if we do so.

After the transactions are confirmed and mined, 12788 DAI will appear in our wallet and 1 WBTC will disappear from our wallet (it will be moved to the vault we create) and we will also lose the Ethereum network fees. 12788 DAI we can use immediately.

Redemption is done in a similar way - we return the DAI, which unlocks the collateral that we withdraw back to our wallet. Everything is done on the same page.

Aave platform on the Avalanche network

We'll try the second example on the Avalanche network, although in the next section we'll show perhaps a slightly better way for this platform and network. However, we'll show this approach in this form mainly because, if we want, the exact same approach works on the Ethereum network as well. You just use ETH instead of AVAX and choose the Ethereum Mainnet. The reason we do this on the Avalanche network is because there are significantly lower fees on it than on the Ethereum network at the time of this writing. Aave supports other networks as well, including Ethereum's layer two protocols.

First, we will add the Avalanche C-Chain network to our Metamask or similar extension [according to the official instructions](). We **always** use Metamask with a hardware wallet. In case that wallet is Ledger, we choose the Ethereum app in the device's interface (not Avalanche) because Avalanche C-Chain is fully compatible with Ethereum.

We get an address from Metamask and try to buy AVAX tokens with Bitcoin Lightning (using sideshift.ai, for example). We choose BTC (Lightning) as the source and AVAX as the target cryptocurrency and enter our address on the AVAX C-chain (it will start with 0x as the Ethereum address):

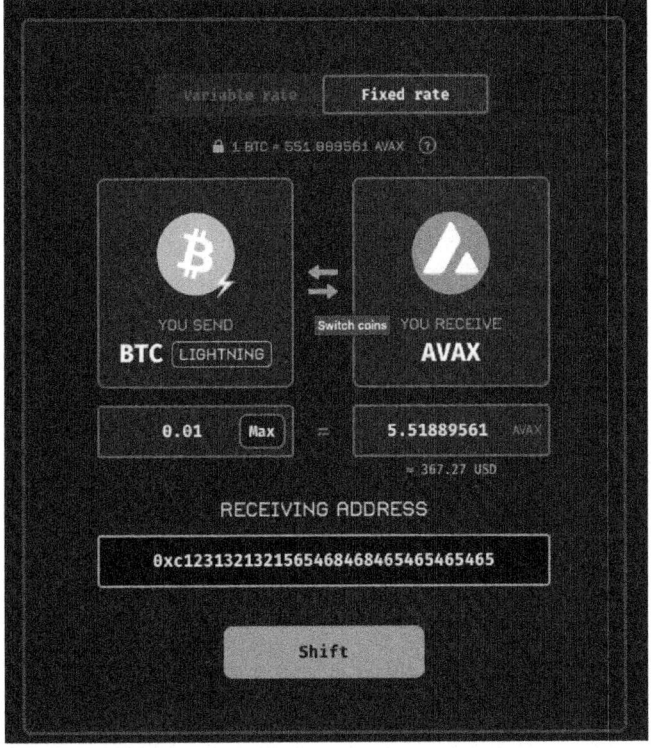

Using the Lightning network will give us a bit more privacy, because there will be no permanent record of the transaction on the Bitcoin network. Since Lightning network has instant finality (confirmation) and the Avax network has finality within one second, both transactions will be confirmed almost instantly.

Now let's buy some WBTC.e to secure the loan. WBTC.e is a form of Bitcoin on the Avalanche network. On the Ethereum network, it will be called WBTC. The reason we buy WBTC.e is because we want to have the collateral denominated in Bitcoin, so we want to stay neutral to the price of Bitcoin. If you want, you can use something else as collateral - for example, wrapped Ethereum (WETH.e on the Avalanche network or simply ETH), or on the Avalanche network, the native AVAX token. For example, let's visit the paraswap.io cryptocurrency meta-exchange. The first thing we need to do is to sign a message that we are not from the US and agree to the terms and conditions (the confirmation will again be on a display of your hardware wallet).

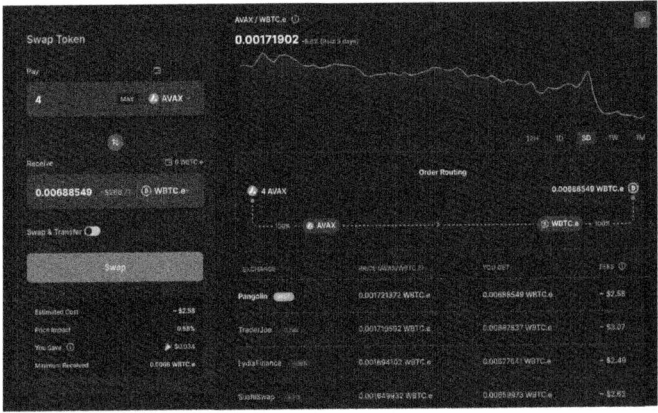

Select the currency (we want to change AVAX to WBTC.e) and enter the amount (in this case 4 AVAX).

On the right, the exchange will find the best way to exchange AVAX for WBTC.e. In this case, Pangolin exchange will give us the best price. In case one exchange does not have enough liquidity at the best price, ParaSwap can also choose a more complex path, exchanging part on one exchange and part on the other. On the next page, we confirm the transaction and sign it with a hardware wallet using Metamask. If we would exchange something other than AVAX, we need to approve the token to be used on Paraswap exchange.

Now we can visit aave.com. Select Launch App to get to the app. First, we select the Avalanche Market network option instead of the Ethereum network (at the time of this writing, the current version is version 3). We select the option to connect a wallet and we will see the dashboard:

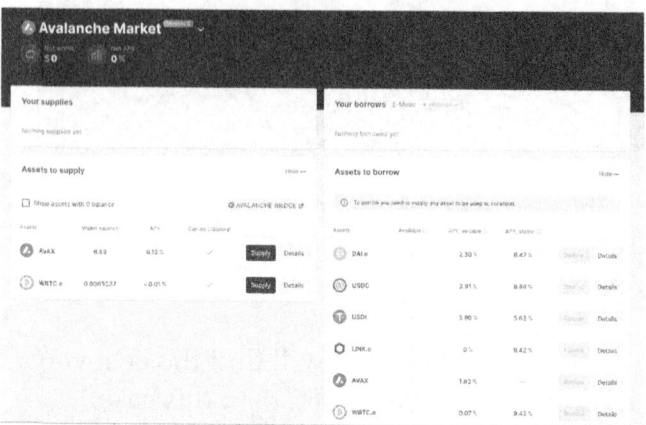

We can see that we have not yet deposited anything (the Your supplies part), we have not borrowed anything (Your borrows), but we can deposit AVAX or WBTC.e. Unlike MakerDAO, we can combine collateral and use a combination of assets (for example, we can deposit both AVAX and WBTC.e at the same time). Let's deposit WBTC.e using the Supply button.

We can click on the text "MAX" to deposit all WBTC.e that we have. This will automatically fill in the amount. The insertion is done in two transactions, first we have to select "Approve to continue" so that Aave can take the WBTC.e and after confirming the transaction with the second transaction we insert the collateral.

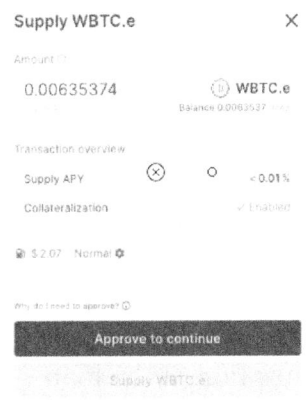

If we want, we can repeat the same procedure with AVAX and we will have two types of collateral (with different interest rates).

Now we can borrow. In the "Assets to borrow" section, we select the stablecoin we want to borrow. There are two things to consider - the interest and the fact that the stablecoin we borrow is also the stablecoin we have to pay back later. In this example, we will borrow the DAI stablecoin (in the form of DAI.e - i.e. a wrapped DAI, bridged from the Ethereum network on the Avalanche C-chain).

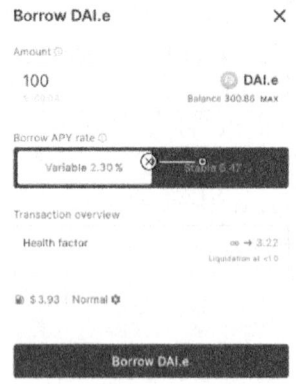

We see that we can borrow 300.86 DAI.e, but we will borrow only 100 to have sufficient collateral in case of market moves. In the next section you will confirm the type of interest. We see that the variable interest is currently 2.30%, but it may change over the course of the loan. Or we can fix the interest at 6.47% for the duration of the loan.

The health factor tells us how safe the loan is relative to the collateral. I recommend calculating the exchange rate of your collateral at which the loan is getting close to liquidation. However, you can only do this if you only have one type of collateral. If you use different types, you can use my tracking script[1] to monitor. However, you need to know your way around the command-line a bit. Or use Aave's health monitoring tool, which you can access from the top menu, near the health factor value.

---

[1] https://github.com/jooray/AAVE_Account_Health_Factor

The health factor will therefore change from "infinity" after this transaction is confirmed (as we have not yet borrowed anything) to 3.22, while a factor less than 1 already results in the liquidation of the collateral.

We can take a final look at the dashboard:

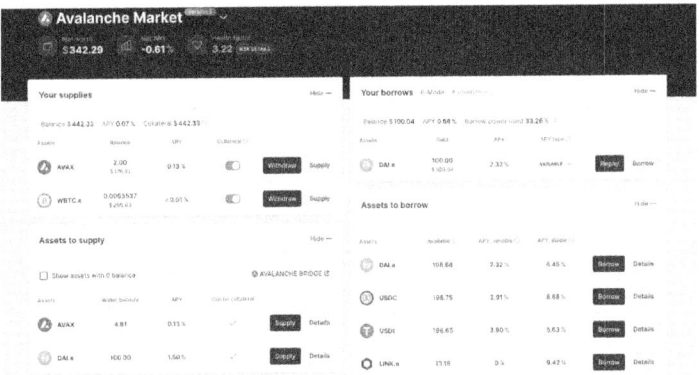

We can see what collateral we have, what interest we have on individual positions and the total interest (part of Net APY). We can also see at any time whether our loan is healthy or needs to be repaid or collateral added in the Health Factor section, where we can also get an accurate loan to value calculation by clicking on it. We can also see our "Net Worth", which is the difference between the collateral and the loan. This is the value we would get if we repaid the loan from the collateral.

Now we can still turn the borrowed DAI.e into something we can use to pay that school, vacation, or utility bill. For example, again ParaSwap to AVAX and via sideshift.ai to Monero, Bitcoin Lightning or anything else we can sell for fiat.

Using the native AVAX Bitcoin bridge

We'll stick with the Aave platform on the Avalanche network because it brings something to the table that can't be done that way in Aave on other platforms at the time of this writing. So far, we've been using a representation of Bitcoin in the form of WBTC or WBTC.e. It's a somewhat cumbersome approach, and it's centralized. WBTC (Wrapped Bitcoin) on the Ethereum network is a representation of Bitcoin using a centralized custodian. Direct "wrapping" of Bitcoin in this case can only be done by certain authenticated entities. WBTC.e is then an Avalanche representation of this Wrapped Bitcoin on Ethereum network. Already complicated, huh? We used exchanges to obtain the representation of Bitcoin. However by using exchanges, we could theoretically trigger something that is considered a tax event by some authorities. In addition, we would trust the security of the WBTC institution (founded by the Kyber, Ren, and BitGo projects), and if we use the representation on the Avalanche network, we also trust the security of the bridge between Ethereum and Avalanche.

However, the Avalanche network has also launched a native bridge between Bitcoin and the Avalanche network (AVAX-C). The need to trust third parties is thus reduced to the security of the BTC.b token (which is what the representation of Bitcoin on the Avalanche network is called) and its bridge, when using the method I am going to show you now. This does not mean that the security is necessarily better - bridges of various protocols have been hacked in the past. On the other hand, some independence from the WBTC token may be beneficial, especially in a time of freezing sanctioned addresses in the Ethereum ecosystem. However, that doesn't mean there isn't a similar risk with this token.

If we want to use the native Bitcoin bridge, we need to replace the Metamask extension with the Google Chrome extension Avalanche Core. After adding the extension, we can link it to the Ledger wallet (unfortunately not Trezor) or create a software wallet. I definitely recommend using a hardware wallet. If we want to create a software wallet, it's a traditional exercise - we write down the seed, verify it, create a wallet name, and choose a password to decrypt the wallet. After clicking on the wallet icon, we can select Bitcoin:

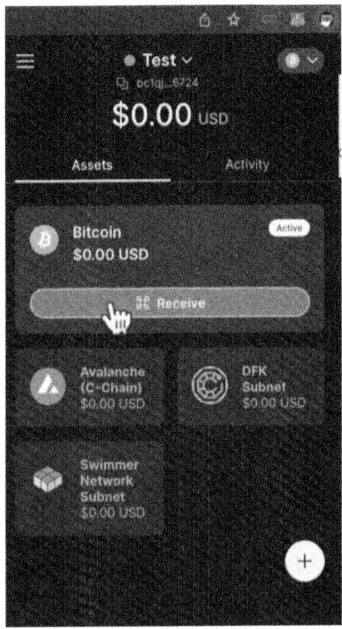

After selecting "Receive", we will see a QR code and the Bitcoin address. This is the address belonging to the wallet we just created (or linked to Ledger). However, a big privacy concern here - since the Bitcoin address and the Avalanche C-Chain address are cryptographically linked (to make the bridge work), this wallet inherits the privacy model from Ethereum technology and thus from the Avalanche C-Chain network.

The wallet always shows the same single address that belongs to a given Avalanche account. Thus, all transactions you make in Bitcoin will be visible at this Bitcoin address, and in addition, the associated Avalanche address can be found from this address. I therefore recommend that you pay more attention to privacy. For example, you can send funds to this address using the swap-out service from Lightning (Breez or Phoenix wallet) or do a thorough coinjoin beforehand (Wasabi, Samourai Wallet, Sparrow Wallet).

After sending Bitcoins to the Core wallet, we can flip them to the BTC.b token on the Avalanche network using the integrated bridge. This can be done by pressing the "+" button on the bottom right:

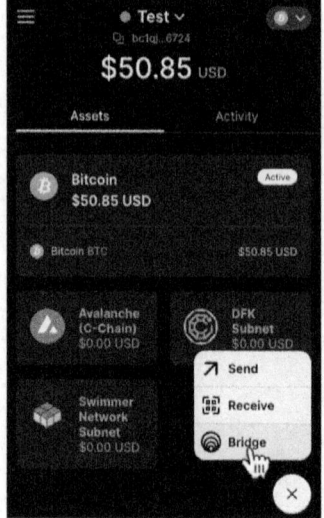

On the next screen we select what we want to bridge (Bitcoin), where to (Avalanche C-Chain) and in what value (the easiest is probably to click "Max", there's not much reason to keep Bitcoins in this wallet).

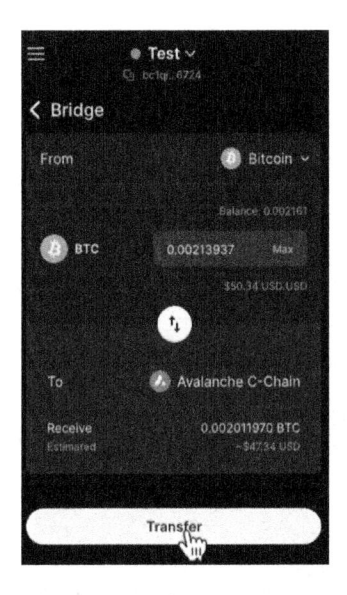

After clicking on "Transfer", a screen will appear where we can see the progress of the bridging - confirmations in the Bitcoin network and, after enough confirmations, the sending of tokens in the Avalanche C-Chain network:

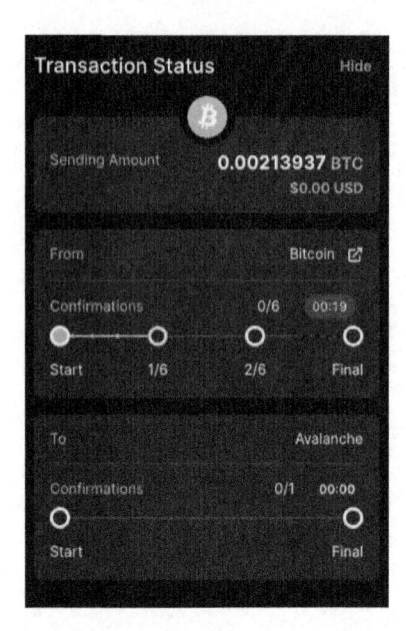

After six confirmations in the Bitcoin network, we will have a balance in our wallet already under the Avalanche tab:

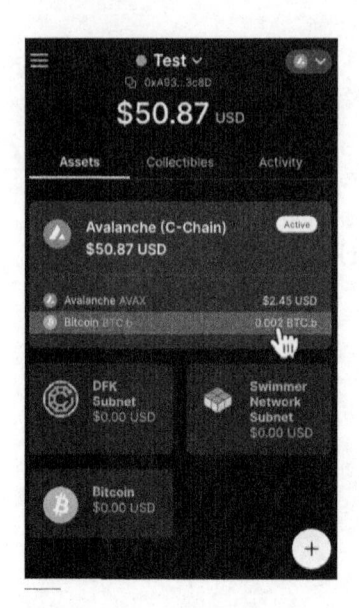

Note that not only have we added Bitcoin BTC.b (which is the wrapped form of our Bitcoins that can be sent on the Avalanche network), but also the AVAX token. This will be added if we send a minimum amount of Bitcoin (currently $75) to a new Avalanche account and is used to allow us to do some minimum amount of transactions on the Avalanche network and have money for fees. However, I recommend adding a bit more AVAX tokens (using Paraswap, for example), as these AVAX tokens for fees will quickly run out - and it's good to have a small stockpile if we need to replenish the collateral or close a position quickly, for example.

Now we can proceed similarly to Aave's WBTC.e, but using the BTC.b token as collateral:

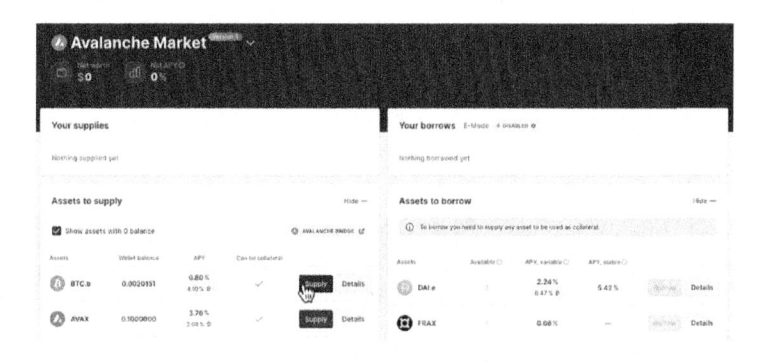

As I write these lines, the supply side is paying over 4% p.a., part of which is a reward from the Avalanche foundation for using their native bridged token. It's a nice bonus, and it's possible that your resulting APY on the loan will be positive because the interest you pay on the loan will be less than the reward for providing the collateral. This situation is of course not a standard market situation and is only possible because the Avalanche project wants to incentivize people to use their DeFi ecosystem. Fortunately, our position is in no way dependent on the value of the AVAX token, it is just good to withdraw the reward from time to time and either exchange it for BTC.b (and replenish the collateral) or use it to repay part of the loan.

For example, if I deposit $40.66 in BTC as collateral and borrow $20 USDC (the procedure is identical to the previous chapter on Aave, except I confirm the transaction in the Core extension and not in Metamask), the resulting position looks like this:

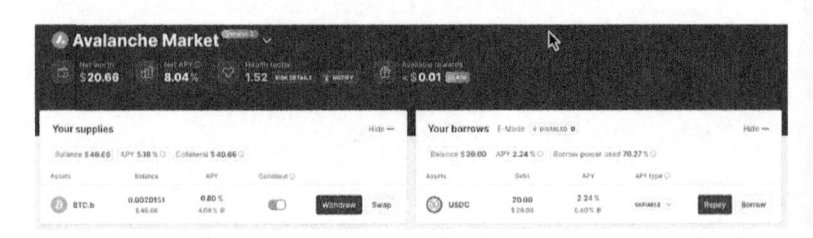

Our Net Worth (the amount of collateral minus the amount of loans) is $20.66. The Net APY in this case is 8.04%, so we receive an annual interest of 8.04% on the amount of the net position (i.e. on $20.66). This is even after factoring in the interest we pay on the loan. This APY depends on current market interest rates and of course the collateral to loan ratio. We haven't accumulated any rewards in this short while, but when we do, we can click the Claim button at the top right under "Available rewards". We can change these rewards, which come in the form of a WAVAX token, via Paraswap to anything we want (like BTC.b and add it as collateral, or USDC and pay back part of the loan - or we can change them to Bitcoins via sideshift).

How can we use the loan? For example, by turning the borrowed USDC back into BTC.b and sending it to the Bitcoin network. Or any other way. We can change USDC to BTC.b via Paraswap, then send them via Bridge from the Core extension:

Repayment is similar - we either use the Repay function and repay the collateral loan (beware, this can be a tax event) or we send USDC to the Avax network and repay the USDC, unlocking the entire collateral.

More efficient position opening with respect to fees

If we don't care about the tax burden (e.g. we live in a country with a lower tax per crypto or we have made a tax loss), it is possible to open this position more efficiently. If we have $3,000 worth of Bitcoins in our hardware wallet and we want to borrow $1,000, we can do what we described above - move the $3,000 to another network (e.g. Avalanche), exchange it for a form of Bitcoin (e.g. WBTC.e), deposit it in a DeFi lending platform (e.g. Aave), borrow $1,000 and convert it to Avax, for example, convert it (e.g. via Sideshift) to Bitcoin, and then sell it - thereby using the $1,000 loan. As we can see, there is too much shifting and changing, which of course costs fees.

At the end of this operation, we have $1000 worth of Bitcoin in a Bitcoin wallet, and we have $3000 worth of Bitcoin collateral and a loan of $1000 on Aave or another lending platform.

However, if at the end we again have $1000 worth of Bitcoin in our wallet. What if we leave it there in the first place?

The simpler way to open the same position is therefore this: Exchange Bitcoins worth only 2000$ for wrapped Bitcoins on the lending platform. Thus, 1000$ will remain in our original wallet in BTC. We put the wrapped Bitcoins (worth 2000$) as collateral, we borrow 1000$. We are now in a more risky position in the short term because the value of our collateral is only twice the value of the loan. But we can exchange the borrowed stablecoins back into wrapped Bitcoins via ParaSwap and put those in back as a collateral.

The resulting position is the same - we have $1000 worth of Bitcoins left in our Bitcoin wallet (which will pay for the consumption we wanted the loan for) and we have collateral worth $3000 (in WBTC or WBTC.e) and a debt in stablecoin of $1000 on the lending platform. But along the way we paid less in exchange fees.

Spark.fi – Aave-like experience with more stable interest rates

In the previous chapters, we explored the intricacies of Oasis Borrow and Aave. Oasis Borrow, a project of MakerDAO, the creators of the DAI stablecoin, is a bit more complex, with its vault system, requiring a nuanced understanding of various conditions for borrowing. This complexity, while robust, stands in stark contrast to Aave's streamlined experience. Aave, with its intuitive user interface, simplifies the borrowing and lending process by clearly displaying types of collateral and borrowable assets alongside their respective interest rates.

However, Aave's variable interest rates, which can sometimes surge to 10%-15% p.a., pose a challenge, especially when compared to the relatively stable, though not entirely fixed, rates of Oasis Borrow. These rates in Oasis are governed by the MKR token holders of MakerDAO, offering a different kind of stability influenced by community governance.

Addressing the gaps between these two platforms, Spark.fi emerges as an innovative solution. It's a community project backed by MakerDAO and using the code of Aave, merging the user-friendly interface of Aave with the stability in borrowing rates akin to Oasis Borrow.

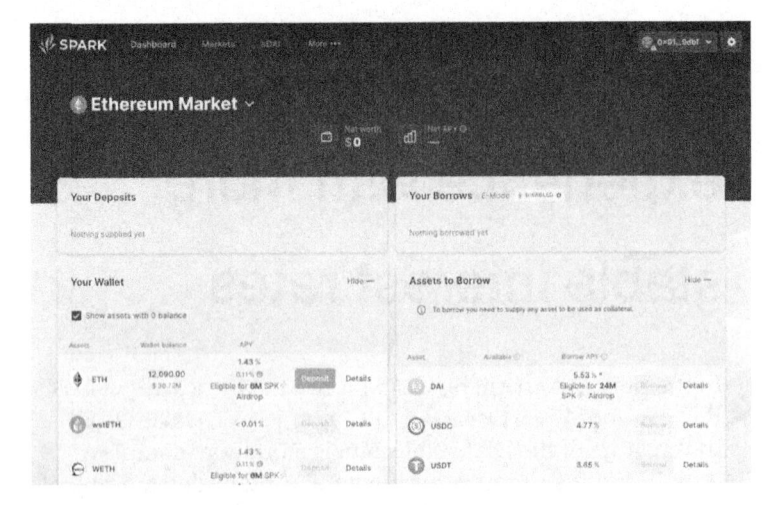

Users can deposit a variety of assets in Spark.fi, such as wrapped BTC and Ethereum, as collateral, and then borrow DAI at a comparatively stable interest rate. An interesting option if you want to deposit Ethereum and not Bitcoin is to change it to staked Ethereum, which earns interest rates from liquid staking. Doing this is out of scope of this course, which is focused on Bitcoin, but it is good to understand that this is an option. Learn more at lido.fi.

We will not show how Spark.Fi works in detail, because we already did – the user interface and borrowing experience is the same as on Aave.

Firefish Platform

While previous platforms serve bitcoiners by using wrapped or bridged Bitcoin, our next platform - Firefish - and its underlying protocol works directly on the bitcoin blockchain. The platform allows you to take out a loan in EUR, USD, or CZK, which will come directly to you via a transfer to your bank account from a counterparty that the platform finds for you. Locking of the collateral is done using the Firefish protocol in the form of a multisig address, which requires signatures of all three of its participants - you as the borrower, and two "oracles". One oracle determines whether fiat was sent to the borrower and, consequently, whether the loan was repaid. The other decides if the liquidation should happen based on the price of Bitcoin. The protocol is designed so that whoever signs the decision cannot directly benefit from signing it - for example, the liquidation decision is just adding a signature to the liquidation transaction, but the liquidator is a different entity - the address is pre-signed in the liquidation transaction and signed also by the borrower.

Once you've created an escrow contract, you even have a pre-signed transaction with a time lock that returns Bitcoins to you. This pre-signed transaction can simply be sent to the bitcoin network in case the platform stops working - so you get your bitcoins back.

The advantage is also a relatively high loan to value parameter - at the time of writing it is 95%, although the initial collateral is usually twice the amount owed.

Firefish is a centralized platform, but the lending is peer to peer - meaning that the counterparty lending you fiat is not Firefish directly, but someone who wants a return on their fiat investment (i.e. a Firefish Earn user) with as little risk as possible. Firefish is therefore a platform that connects investors and borrowers and allows you to create and enforce a loan and escrow contract.

It also differs from other platforms in that the loan is in the form of fiat currency in the banking system - the borrowed euros, dollars (or Czech crowns) arrive directly from the counterparty to your bank account. This of course has consequences for your privacy, the counterparty knows your name, address and account number. I assume the platform will also introduce more detailed KYC.

While the need for KYC is a big drawback from my point of view, bank transfers can often be unexpectedly useful - if you want to buy a property, it can be quite problematic to convert a large amount of stablecoins (a form of fiat currency) into a balance in your bank account that you can use to pay for the property. Even if you can use the services of an exchange, an incoming transfer of a larger amount from a cryptocurrency exchange can raise questions with the bank or outright cause the transaction to be blocked or even your account to be closed. Banks really don't like larger amounts from exchanges. In the case of Firefish, however, the loan comes directly from the counterparty you are borrowing from, and you can prove to the bank that it is a loan.

How to open a loan through Firefish

First you need to register on the platform. There may be a waitlist, but the wait is not long and you should be able to access the platform within a week. After selecting "Firefish Cash" in the menu, click "I want to borrow" to enter your loan requirements:

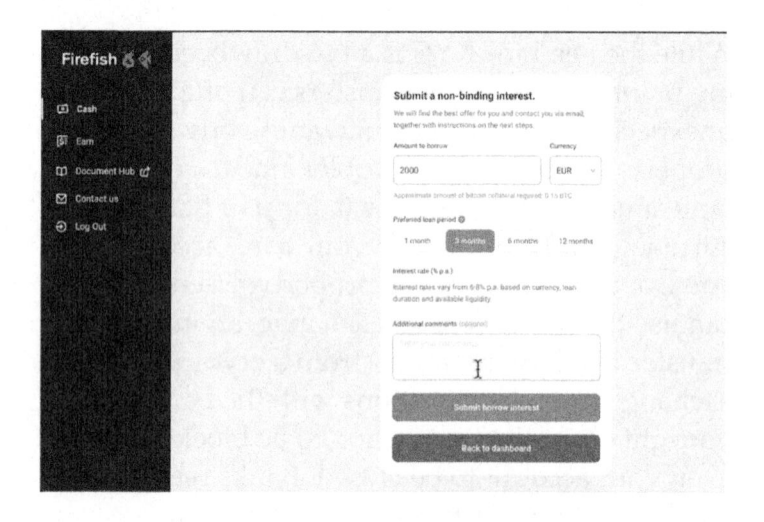

You can choose the amount, currency and duration of the loan. Once entered, you will see the loan tab where you can see the next steps and the parameters of the loan:

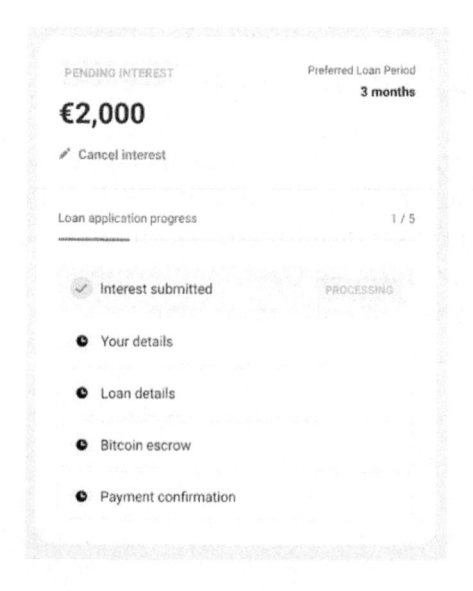

Now wait for the offer email:

Firefish

New Firefish deal

Dear member,

thank you again for your interest in Firefish!

We have received your Firefish Cash interest, through which you lock your Bitcoin and receive cash.

An investor is ready for you with the following terms:

Period: 3 months
Loan Amount: 2.000 EUR
Interest Rate: 6.0% p.a.
Amount Due: 2.030 EUR

If you agree with the terms, please, let us know! We would then proceed with setting up the deal.

If you have any questions, please don't hesitate to contact us at hello@firefish.io!

If we want to accept this offer, we simply reply to the email and wait for the next email when the contract is ready for us.

The next step will be to fill in the details that are required for the bank transfer and locking of the collateral. The required data are currently name, address and payment details - account number, bank, etc. The personal details must match with the account owner, as this is the basis on which the investor will enter the payment order.

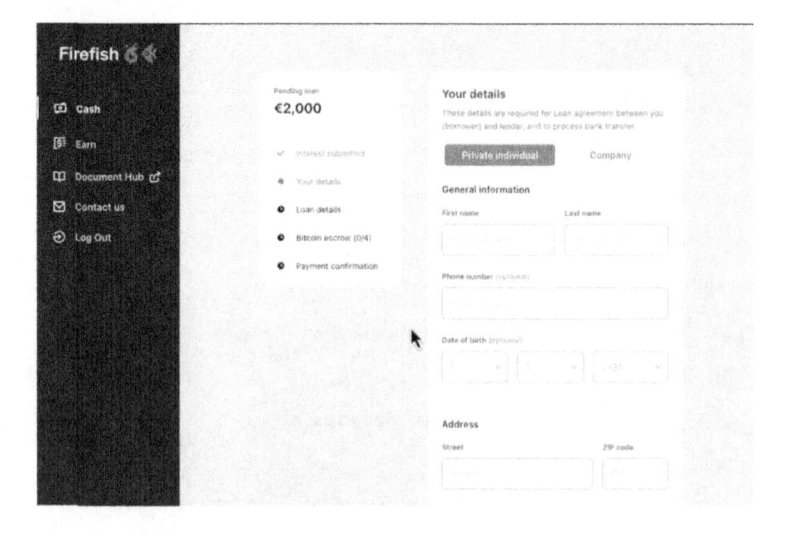

After confirming the details once again, this time you will see the exact details of the loan - opening date, expiry date, amount owed, interest and so on. It's time to lock your Bitcoins. To lock Bitcoins, Firefish creates temporary private keys in your browser and stores them encrypted on the Firefish server as well. Therefore, Firefish will again verify that you know your password, because without it, you wouldn't be able to access the private keys if something happens while you're locking Bitcoins and you need to use the option to return the Bitcoins.

Next, you enter the Bitcoin address where you want to return the Bitcoins - either in case of failure of setup, or in case you repay the loan:

Importantly, this address must exist and be under your full control for the duration of the loan. Since the Firefish protocol works on the basis of partially pre-signed transactions, it is not possible to change this address later. Therefore, I recommend using your hardware wallet address. Do not to type a deposit address of an exchange there under any circumstances!

In the next step, we will be shown a classic Bitcoin on-chain payment QR code and the address and amount in text form as well. We have to send coins to this address in the exact amount as requested by the platform.

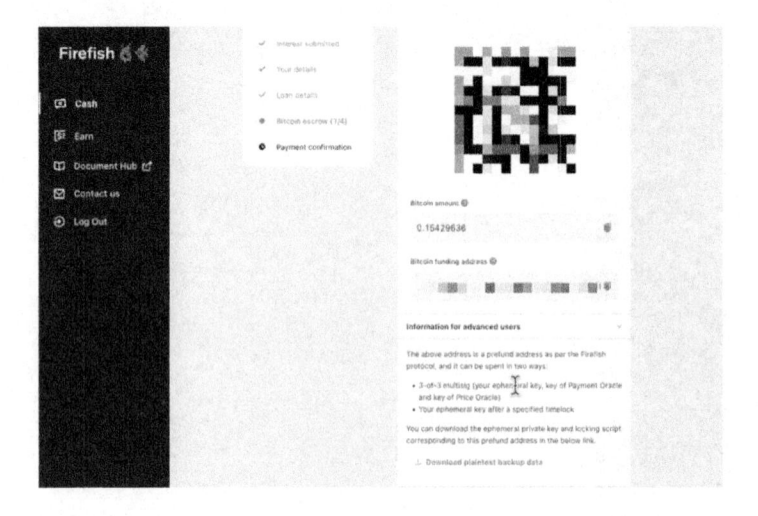

This address is a "prefund" address, so it is not an address where your Bitcoins will remain locked. This is because the necessary partially signed transactions need to be done based on knowledge of a specific UTXO. Funds from this address can be spent in two ways - either by using multisig 3-of-3, or after a certain amount of time, when you can also withdraw Bitcoins using only your temporary key. This key can also be downloaded locally to your computer in the "Information for advanced users" section. The important part here is that without your consent, these coins cannot be moved by Firefish - you only add your signature to an escrow transaction, once you have all signed transactions, including the recovery transaction.

The next step is for Firefish's payment oracle to create transactions that deposit Bitcoins to the escrow address created (i.e., the address where the collateral will be stored) and pre-sign all the necessary transactions they are supposed to sign - including a time-locked transaction that will return Bitcoins to you in case something happens.

Once the transactions are pre-signed, you will receive another email and can complete the escrow lock-in. You can download the signed recovery transaction first, and then you can continue with the setup.

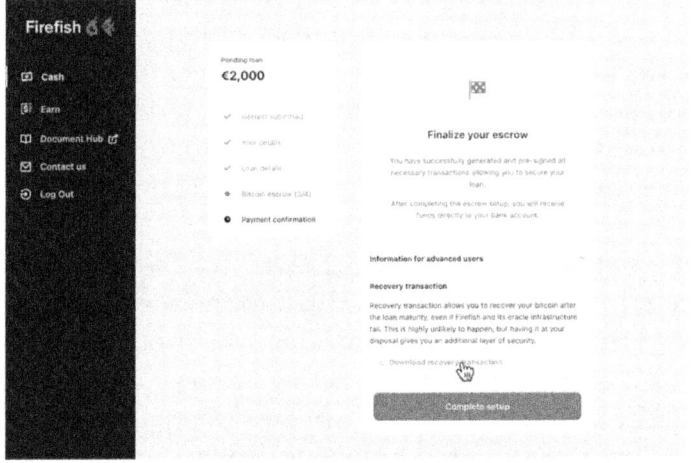

The recovery transaction is in a standard format and contains all three required signatures. This is how its details look like in Sparrow Wallet:

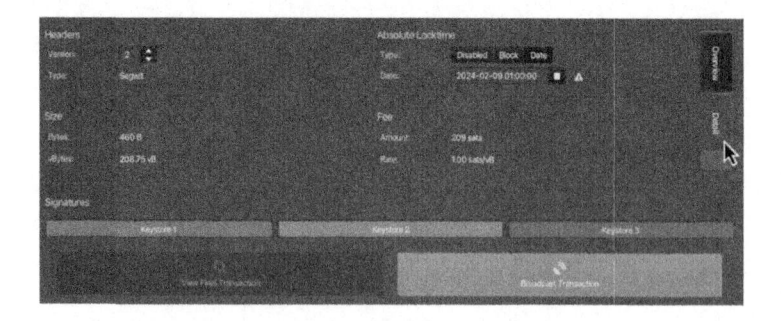

We can see that it has all three signatures, you can send it straight to the network (using the "Broadcast Transaction" button) and it will return your Bitcoins to you. Of course, the transaction is only valid after 2/9/2024, which in this case is a month after the loan is due. That's plenty of time to decide whether you've repaid the loan or whether it should possibly be liquidated. However, if the platform were to stop functioning, for example, you can still get your Bitcoins.

The only thing left to do is to wait for the fiat (2000 EUR in this case) to be credited to the account and confirmed on the platform. Once the funds are received, the loan is fully active. In the credit tab, you can view the loan documents (loan agreement and short summary), add collateral in case of a significant drop in Bitcoin value, re-download the recovery transaction, request early repayment, or add the maturity date to your calendar (in the form of an .ics file):

ACTIVE LOAN		Maturity Date
€2,000		**9 Jan 2024**
Loan actions ▼		Interest Rate
		6.0 %
📄 View loan documents		
↑ Top-up collateral		
⬇ Save recovery transaction		
$ Request early repayment		0.15419 BTC
		€13,860
📅 Add maturity event to calendar		9 Oct 2023
Days Left ❓		91
Amount due ❓		€2,030

Congratulations, you borrowed fiat in peer-to-peer mode.

Advantages and disadvantages of the Firefish platform

Unlike DeFi platforms, in Firefish you lose privacy and interact with a traditional banking system, although the platform plans to add stablecoin support over time. Both the platform and the counterparty know your identity, which is unavoidable in the case of a bank transfer.

On the other hand, a bank transfer can also be an advantage - the loan is easy to document. This can be particularly useful if you borrowed as a legal entity, for example to finance the operation of your business. It can also be advantageous if you are borrowing a larger amount that you need to get into a bank account (for example, to buy a property) and the bank may not like a transfer from a bitcoin exchange.

The peer-to-peer nature is also an important difference from many smart contract-based platforms. Smart contracts pool investor funds, which are then lent out, with both investors and borrowers having a relationship with the smart contract and therefore the entire 'pool'. This means that a possible bug in a smart contract or a systemic problem will very likely affect all users of the platform, or at least of the particular pool. In the case of the Firefish platform, the contracts are separated, and the collateral locked in different addresses with different keys. All possible loan situations that can occur are created at the beginning when the contract is set up, and are immutable. Therefore, it is unlikely that a bug in the platform or a hacking attack on the platform will cause a loss of Bitcoins. On the other hand, the platform processes, holds, and can release the personal data of both investors and borrowers upon request (for example with a warrant).

Another difference is the fixed interest rate for the duration of the loan. This can be both an advantage and a disadvantage, depending on the needs of investors and borrowers and the current market interest rates.

The advantage for Europeans is that the platform supports euros (and Czech crowns) in addition to dollars and supports local bank transfers through the SEPA system. When looking at the quality of fiat currencies, the dollar is the clear king - the global reserve currency, that is trusted by the most people. But in the case of a loan, this is a disadvantage - you want to borrow something that is losing value faster than the increase in the amount owed due to interest. In addition, if you earn euros (or Czech crowns), when you borrow dollars you run the additional risk that the value of the money you earn to use to repay the loan will be lower due to the loss in value of these fiat currencies against the dollar. Therefore, being able to borrow in an "inferior" fiat currency - euros or Czech crowns - can be advantageous.

Among the drawbacks is that Firefish is a relatively new platform, where, for example, it is not yet clear how it will be possible to do a roll-over of the loan if you want to extend it for a longer period than originally agreed. And whether it will survive the start-up phase and the more difficult phases of the business.

Bitcoin futures

We can also simulate a loan using Bitcoin futures. There we can fix the interest rate or use variable interest. We can use a derivative exchange without KYC - even one of the DeFi exchanges. This chapter uses ByBit as an example, but since it introduced mandatory KYC, I do not recommend it anymore. Pick some other one (after thorough). I try to maintain a list of them on the List of Derivative Exchanges[2] page, so make sure to check for the latest updates.

Bitcoin futures are designed to buy and sell Bitcoin in the future at a pre-agreed on rate. If we don't want to sell Bitcoins but want to enjoy them, we can do so, for example, by buying a derivative settled at a future date and selling the Bitcoins we have today. The goal is to have a similar amount of Bitcoins at the end of this operation (when we "pay off the loan to ourselves") as at the beginning. However, the tax implications of this operation are not as pleasant as for a real loan (check with your accountant).

---

[2] https://juraj.bednar.io/en/list-of-derivative-exchanges/

We will add collateral after you register for the exchange. Since we are going to buy future Bitcoin (we are long Bitcoin against USD), we need to give collateral to the exchange in case the Bitcoin price drops. This is because the Bitcoin future we use (called the Inverse future) is settled in Bitcoin and thus settlement occurs in Bitcoin - we will explain this later. So let's imagine that we want to borrow $1000. Unlike a DeFi loan, we only need collateral for a possible exchange rate fluctuation against us (i.e. down), let's say by a third. So we send BTC worth, say, $600 to the exchange as collateral. Why so much? Because we hold the collateral in BTC, and if it falls by a third, we'll have to make up the $333 loss, but our Bitcoins worth $600 today will only be worth $396. Collateral is not converted to dollars in the case of inverse futures, it stays in Bitcoins (HODL!).

Let's try to pick a fixed future for September 2022:

So we chose the BTCUSD0930 Inverse Future, which expires on the 30th of September. Thus, we are entering into a contract to buy Bitcoin in the future at the current rate. The rate that Bybit is offering us is 39720 USD/BTC, but the spot price is 39023 USD/BTC. There are 200 days until expiration, so we will pay about 3.25% p.a. The advantage is that if we enter this position and close it at expiration, we have the interest rate locked in for the duration.

How do we do it? We enter a Market order of 1000 USD and click Buy / Long:

Now we can sell $1000 of our other Bitcoins (that's the "loan") any way we want.

When the expiration time comes, we simply buy Bitcoins for $1000 at the price at the time of the expiry. If the Bitcoin exchange rate is higher, the short side of this trade will pay us the difference and we will have almost the same amount of Bitcoins as we started with. The Bitcoins will appear in the wallet where we had collateral - they will be added to the collateral. If we add up the amount of Bitcoins we added with the ones we bought at the current exchange rate of $1000, we have almost the same amount of Bitcoin. Why almost? Because we bought Bitcoins at a slightly worse rate than we sold them (the difference between the future price and the spot price, that's where the interest rate shows up). This difference can also be negative (in which case the futures market is essentially paying us to borrow), although this situation doesn't occur often. If the future price is higher than the spot price, we say the market is in contango, if the future is cheaper than the spot, it is called backwardation. We see how much we pay or get paid when we enter the position (by observing the difference between spot and future price) - settlement at expiration already occurs at the current spot price.

If the price of Bitcoin drops at expiration time, we will have less collateral on the exchange than we sent there. But that doesn't matter, because we'll buy more Bitcoins for $1000, so we'll have almost the same amount of USD we started with again.

63

Collateral on the derivatives exchange should be monitored from time to time. Or we can make a note of the liquidation price. In a fluctuation we can lose both collateral and open loan position, so it's not a good risk to take.

The risk of this trade is, of course, also in the exchange itself. However, decentralised derivatives exchanges are also gradually improving and therefore, over time, it may be better to trust a smart contract rather than a third party.

On expiry, you can go straight into a new position (and therefore "renew" your loan) on the current terms at that time.

If you don't feel like renewing your loan for a fixed time, you can also enter a perpetual swap, which "renews automatically" every 8 hours. However, the way it is financed is similar to a variable rate and the interest rates can be wild. In this case, it may be wise to lock in a low enough interest rate, and only use perpetual swaps if we don't know how long we want the loan for or if the interest is too high.

As a reminder, you can only lock in interest on futures with expiration if you hold out until expiration. If you need to exit the position early, this is of course possible (you use the Sell/Short of the same amount), but you may pay the difference in futures price versus spot for this early exit, which may be higher than when you entered the position.

Futures using 10101 app

10101 is an **experimental** bitcoin wallet with an integrated futures exchange that offers a perpetual swap renewed weekly. It's perfect for trying out this futures-based approach to borrowing. It is a wallet that is based on the Discreet Log Contracts technology integrated in a payment channel. The downside is that it's a relatively new project, in beta.

In 10101, everything is represented by Bitcoins, which we fund through the Bitcoin network. This opens a direct channel between us and the platform. Thus, unlike the lending platforms we mentioned (MakerDao, Aave), we don't use any tokens. At the same time, unlike centralized exchanges, we do not send Bitcoins to a third party, but they remain in a channel to which we have private keys. This reduces the number of third parties we have to trust. However, the user interface still has gaps, as it is a new project.

After installing the app, we can tap on the Receive button and get a QR code and address to fund the wallet. Note that these coins will be used as margin, so we do not have to fund the whole position size.

Address
bc1q39856u82vgsvuy2y5a52rc24vt2vrxa6d52ksm

Of course it's a good idea to back up your wallet. When you click on Backup Wallet, you get the classic 12 words mnemonic, like any other wallet. You need to write these words down to make the backup. I would note that the backup scheme is not standard, because no other wallet can recover DLC channels.

Once paid, we have a classic Bitcoin wallet in which we can send and receive on-chain payments. However, what we will be more interested in is the Trade tab where we can enter futures positions:

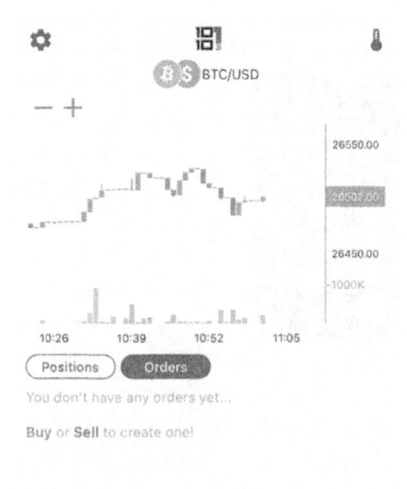

Let's take out a $10 futures-based loan. We enter a Market order for Buy (green button) of 10 USD. We see different leverage options - from 1x to 5x. These tell us when our position will be liquidated and how much "margin" (collateral) we need.

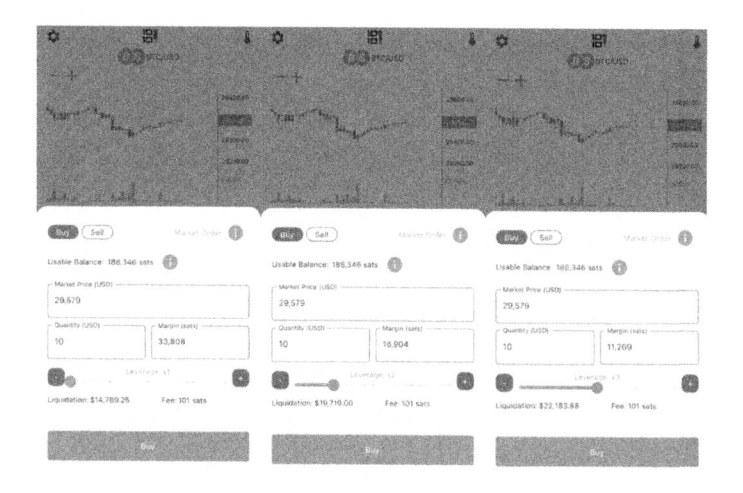

At no leverage ("x1") the position is liquidated if Bitcoin falls to $14789.25 and we need a margin of 33808 sats, at leverage "x2", we get liquidated at a price of $19719, and we need a margin of 16904 sats. Finally, at at leverage "x3" the position is liquidated at a price of $22183.88 and we need a margin of only 11269 sats. So here we choose the size of the collateral needed vs when we need to "take care" of the "loan" - what price must bitcoin fall to for us to need to add additional collateral.

The only thing we choose with the leverage is when we have to add collateral, or at what price the exchange will close our order. Beware that our possible Bitcoin payoff is also limited by the margin and size of the channel – this will be important during rapid rise of the price of Bitcoin.

We are not really doing a "leveraged trade" though - after returning $10 (i.e. buying Bitcoin at $10 at the current price and closing the position), we get the same amount of BTC as before, minus fees and interest.

After setting leverage and clicking on "Buy", we need to open a DLC channel – we have just funded the wallet, but the channel is not open yet.

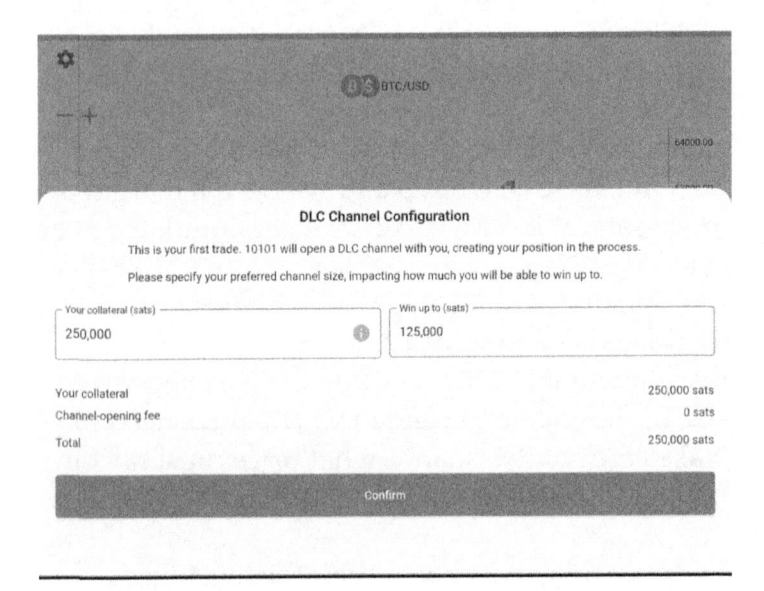

DLC Channel Configuration

This is your first trade. 10101 will open a DLC channel with you, creating your position in the process.

Please specify your preferred channel size, impacting how much you will be able to win up to.

Your collateral (sats)	Win up to (sats)
250,000	125,000

Your collateral — 250,000 sats
Channel-opening fee — 0 sats
Total — 250,000 sats

Confirm

After confirming, we have entered a long position on BTC/USD, which can be viewed as a form of borrowing. The position then looks like this in the interface (I selected the "x2" leverage):

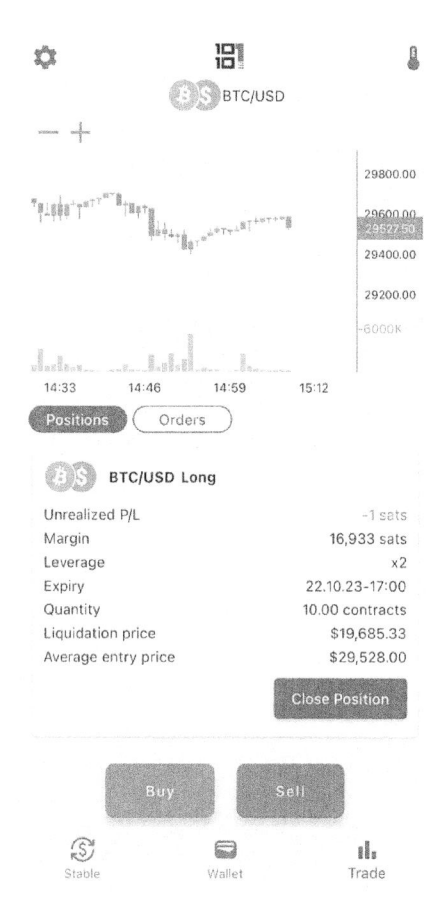

We see again the liquidation price ($19685.33), the average entry price, and the margin. This position expires on 10/22/2023 at 5:00 PM, which is Sunday. If we want to extend the position, we need to do it over the weekend, by opening the app. The app should also send us a notification about this.

If we want to use this position as a loan, we should now sell Bitcoins worth $10 on the market - these will become the fiat amount borrowed. Of course we don't need to sell it for dollars, we can directly buy what we need the loan for for Bitcoin.

When we want to "pay back" the loan, we buy Bitcoins for $10 (whatever the exchange rate in the future is) and press the "Close Position" button. The balance of the position plus the newly purchased Bitcoins will total the original amount of Bitcoins (minus fees and interest):

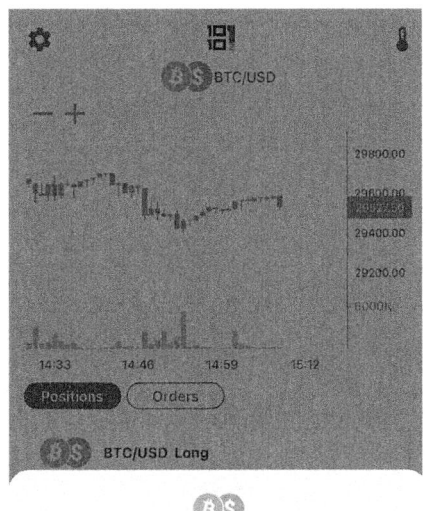

You may have noticed that the liquidation price is falling slower than the margin. This is due to the fact that in this case we have collateral in Bitcoin, the value of which decreases along with the price of Bitcoin. Thus, the decline is cumulative. If Bitcoin falls by half, the value of the collateral (which is in Bitcoin) also falls by half. This is good to keep in mind when planning your positions that are collateralized in Bitcoin.

10101 is an experimental, decentralized wallet and futures exchange without KYC. It's currently in beta, so I recommend it mainly for understanding bitcoin futures and for playing around.

When to repay the loan?

You may be thinking that not selling Bitcoins is just delaying the inevitable - the repayment of the loan will wait for us. But we don't have to repay the loan. We have no monthly repayments, only a growing amount owed – principal and outstanding interest. We have three reasons for not repaying the loan right away.

The first is inflation - if our personal price inflation (i.e. the weighted percentage increase in the prices of those products and services we buy) is higher than the interest rate, there is no reason to repay the loan. If, for example, our personal price inflation is 10% p.a., (whatever the Bureau of Statistics calculates from the prices of bread, tomatoes, beef, rent, and gasoline) but we can borrow at 3%, then we have real negative interest, i.e. we have to pay back money that is less valuable to us than the products and services we spent it on when we borrowed it. This condition has one small but significant "but" - we are borrowing dollars, so we are interested in price increases in dollars, not in euros or any other currency.

The second reason for not repaying the loan may be our expectation of collateral value growth. If we believe that our collateral will grow in value faster than the interest rate (after accounting for dollar inflation), it is worth more to purchase more of the collateral, or just not use it to repay the loan.

The third reason is to assess the tax situation. We basically have two ways to repay the loan - either we earn the money to repay the loan or we use the collateral to repay the loan. The first way is obviously fine, but we need to have the additional income. The second way is a taxable event in many countries, plus we commit the sin of selling our precious Bitcoins.

So we can think of a loan as a credit card that accrues interest, but we don't have to pay it back at any particular point in time - we don't even have to make any minimum repayments. The interest rate can be relatively low because we have good quality collateral with a value well in excess of the loan.

But what can happen (apart from technical, security risks) is that interest rates rise. Since interest is market-determined, there may be a situation where interest rates rise so much that it is not worth borrowing.

Risks and how to deal with them

Like everything, a collateralized loan has its risks. There are known risks and unknown risks (the ones we don't know about in advance and can't even imagine). So, I will describe only the risks known to me and conclude with a question on how to deal with the unknown ones.

When to use a collateralized loan

We expose ourselves to risks because we expect a benefit. That is why I will start with when to even consider a collateralized loan. For example, it may be when we have sufficient collateral against the loan. What is sufficient is individual, but it must be considered that if the value of the collateral decreases, we must either partially repay the loan or replenish the collateral. At the same time, be aware that the position (exchange rate value) needs to be monitored, so this will require our attention. You know the saying, "It's best to take out a loan if you don't **need** it". That is, when a loan is just one option among others to finance your consumption or investment.

To me, good uses are financing consumption or better yet investment, for which we would have to otherwise sell cryptocurrencies. Selling cryptocurrencies often has tax consequences and at the same time we have less cryptocurrencies - which is often a sad experience for a HODLer. But since you need collateral for a collateralized loan, you don't really "need" it - you have another option and that is to sell your crypto. You're not really "in the red", you're just more confident that cryptocurrencies will retain value compared to fiat. "Long crypto, short fiat".

The other good use, in my opinion, is to buy Bitcoin (soft leverage) when the price of Bitcoin is good, we would like to buy anonymously, but all the options around us (like anonymous OTC exchangers) do not have liquidity and no one is selling. Buying Bitcoin and waiting for liquidity to return to the peer-to-peer market around us is a good use-case of collateralized loan. When the liquidity returns, we buy back the stablecoin we borrowed and pay back the loan.

We should not take risks when it is not profitable for us and it is up to you to understand them and evaluate the profitability of a risky investment, I can only teach you about technology. Each person's risk perception is different and individual.

Risk coverage

We cover risks primarily in terms of impact. In traditional risk management, the second component of risk is the probability that a given risk situation will occur, but I think that the estimation of that is so flawed that I just ignore the probability and don't look at what the chance is that the situation will occur. I only consider what is the worst thing that could happen. That means I consider the probability to be near 100% and only look at the impact. As we can easily estimate the impact, this is a strategy that will reduce risk estimation errors.

Although you will find many risks in this section, they can often be covered by one or two strategies. For example, we can cover stablecoin risk and fiat risk at the same time.

The simplest strategy to cover the risk is by being aware of it and accepting it. This is not always possible, but if we go into a risk whose worst-case scenario would not hurt us very much and we can live with it, we may not need to do anything more. That's why it's a good idea to write down such a worst-case scenario and understand what it would mean. If it does not have a significant negative impact on our lives (for example, it is significantly less than our total net worth), we may not even need to do anything.

We rarely cover risks by having a specific strategy for each risk. It is better to look at risks broadly across impact. Nevertheless, we will list the most significant risks that a crypto-collateralized loan has.

Counterparty risk

In crypto collateralized lending, we have different forms of counterparty risk. If it is a centralised platform, it can often be hacked or go bankrupt. This has happened several times in history (e.g. the Celsius platform). Therefore, if we opt for a centralised platform, it is a good idea to prefer a derivatives platform, where we can manage the risk for the duration of the position and only need to have collateral on the exchange to cover downward movements. It doesn't even have to cover the whole loan, just a small amount to start with.

Platform hacks can also occur with decentralised platforms. In addition, the platform may do rehypothecation in a way that is not secure. I recommend asking questions such as whether the platform has a long history, whether it has independent security audits, a bug bounty program, and what it does with collateral - if it lends it, whether it can be verified to whom and whether those to whom it is lent have sufficient backing.

Collateral value and flash crash

If there is a situation where the value of the collateral drops to the point where we reach a level where our position is at risk of being liquidated, do we have a plan? The plan may be to repay the loan, to replenish the collateral, or to accept a loss. When the position is liquidated, we don't have to return anything back, so it may not be as bad as it seems at first glance. Do we know if we are paying a penalty and at what price will the collateral be liquidated? Do we have a plan at what price we will voluntarily close the position and bear the loss of the collateral? If we borrowed in a situation where we would have had to sell the bitcoin anyway, maybe it's not so bad - we may lose the crypto, but we wouldn't have had it without the position anyway. Of course, since the collateral must be worth more than the loan, we risk more units of the collateral than just by selling it.

A plan for flash crashes can also be to buy options that can cover the loss or supplement our collateral. Or simply open a "buy order" to buy the fiat at a low price - we may lose the crypto in the collateral, but we will buy new crypto for a better price at the same time. In any case, it's good to have a "what to do if..." plan.

Interest rate risk

If we don't fix the interest rate, it may grow to a value that we are not comfortable with. Short term interest can go up to hundreds of percent p.a., but that's not necessarily a problem. But when interest rates rise over the long term, it's also a good idea to have a plan. It could be switching to a different product or platform, moving from Defi to futures or vice versa. The position can also be closed in the extreme case of high interest - not because the value of the collateral falls, but because the amount owed rises due to interest.

Stablecoin risk

This risk only applies to us if we use DeFI platforms and borrow stablecoins. Futures that are settled in Bitcoin do not have this problem.

Since we are "short fiat" (we are borrowing fiat, which is a short position), there is no problem if the price of the stablecoin goes down below the peg value. If we borrowed DAI, for example, the best that can happen to us is a crash in the value of DAI. Imagine if it couldn't maintain its peg to the dollar and sold for $0.5. In that case, we could pay off the entire loan for half the dollar value! This also applies to the fall in the value of the dollar itself.

So, the problems of stablecoin would have to be of a different nature to cause us a problem. For example, it could be the non-functionality of the stablecoin itself (for example if transfers stopped working for some reason), a price increase (for example, if DAI traded at $1.2), or a liquidity problem (we could not get enough of it to pay off the loan). Moreover, these problems would have to be long-term.

Fiat value risk

If we borrow dollars, but we planned to repay the loan with earnings denominated in another fiat currency, there may be a problem of the dollar strengthening against the other currency. Hedging fiat value is a product that can be bought in the market. While the dollar is an inflationary fiat currency that is steadily losing value, it may be that other fiat currencies are losing value faster. The dollar is perhaps the best of the bad fiat currencies. Do we have that risk covered?

If we plan to repay the loan from the growth in Bitcoin's value, by selling Bitcoin in the future, we don't necessarily have to cover this risk.

Collateral risk

If we use Bitcoins wrapped in DeFI, this collateral must work. The coins must be wrapped, there should be no error in the bridge between networks or in the wrapping mechanism.

If we use a derivatives exchange, we should be aware of the risk that for some reason we may not be able to withdraw the collateral, even if it is denominated in Bitcoin.

KYC risk

If we are using centralized derivatives exchanges, it is possible that the exchanges will implement KYC once the position is opened. Most of the time they do this so that you have enough time to move the position somewhere else where they don't require KYC (for example, to a decentralized derivatives platform). As a reminder, I maintain a list of current derivative platforms without KYC on my website[3].

However, they might introduce KYC requirements right away and the exchange might not allow Bitcoin withdrawals without identity verification. Therefore, I recommend managing this risk by not having too much collateral on the exchange and rather topping it up when necessary. Or using decentralised derivative platforms.

---

[3] https://juraj.bednar.io/en/list-of-derivative-exchanges/

Risk of network fees

Non-zero risk is also the risk of increased fees from the network on which the loan is taken out. Historically on Ethereum, for example, fees to close a loan or add collateral have been as high as hundreds of dollars (denominated in the native ETH currency in which gas fees are paid, of course).

The same can happen in the Bitcoin network, where just sending Bitcoins to replenish collateral or close a position can be very expensive in the future.

In the normal use of these protocols for simple payments, we can often deal with a high fee situation just by waiting (whether for a weekend in the case of a shorter-term fee spike, or for several weeks or months to deal with a special situation, such as an increase in demand for block space). In the case of a loan, we sometimes may not have enough time and need to pay the fees to put a transaction into the block in the order of hours or days.

Banking network and fiat infrastructure risk

If we've been in Bitcoin longer, it's easy to forget that the fiat world doesn't always work the way we want it to. It is possible that we make a bank transfer and some bank along the way rejects it or wants some additional documentation for the transaction, or to suddenly investigate the source of funds. If we urgently need to replenish collateral, and are waiting for a transfer to an exchange, or need to repay a loan on time through the banking network, it is possible that this may not be possible thanks to the banking network, which does not work as reliably as Bitcoin.

Unknown risks and worst-case scenarios

If we took out a loan for good reasons (for me, for example, the need to sell Bitcoin if I didn't take it out), it's a good idea to look at those risks and other risks we may not know about in advance and look at worst-case scenarios. If the whole loan goes bad, what's the worst that could happen?

With unknown risks, there is no point in assessing the probability - we don't even know what the risks are, let alone the probability with which they will occur. The best we can do with unknown risks is to limit their impact.

The impact is that we lose all the collateral, but we don't have to pay back the loan (the platforms don't know who we are, so we can't owe more than we "locked up" as collateral). Are we okay with this situation? If not, have we done anything to protect ourselves in this situation? Hedging, options, withdrawing excess collateral are examples of what we could do.

Another possibility is that we have an amount that is small enough relative to the rest of the portfolio, but we still don't want to sell Bitcoins. So even a full loss of collateral is not a problem for us - what we wanted to buy, we bought, and we don't lose much of our net worth in case we lose the whole collateral.

Nassim Nicholas Taleb (famous for his book „Black Swan" that talks about unknown risks) said: "Do not measure the risks you are taking, take only risks you understand". I recommend that you open a collateralized loan position only after you understand all the risks and have them covered by your strategy.

How to use the loan

By borrowing, we acquire stablecoin or Bitcoin in a "hedged position" in the case of futures. The first thing most people think of when they want to use a loan is to exchange it for fiat. This is ideally done using a non-KYC crypto dealer or a friend. This is obviously a good solution, but it is not the only solution. First we need to answer the question "What do we want to use the loan for?".

If we just want to buy more Bitcoins with the borrowed money (for example, if we want to do dollar cost averaging without KYC), we can just use an exchange like SideShift, Fixedfloat, or use the Invity metaexchange search engine, or the privacy and private exchange-focused Incognito Wallet, to exchange coins for Bitcoin. In the case of futures, we don't even need to do anything, just open a position. This use is essentially leveraged trading, which can be useful. The "borrow stablecoins and buy Bitcoin" and "open leveraged long position on BTC/fiat" is mathematically the same thing.

However, paying with cryptocurrency is also ideal if you're taking out a loan for something else. You can use Bitrefill to buy coupons for Amazon, Airbnb, Uber or Uber Eats, or top up some mobile prepaid programs.

You may also prefer services where you can pay directly with Bitcoins. For example, you can use Travala for flights and hotels. For more information on how you can use Bitcoin or newly borrowed stablecoins, I recommend my book Cryptocurrencies – Hack your way to a better life. Of course you can buy it with (borrowed fiat turned into) Bitcoin.

Conclusion

We do not sell Bitcoins. Not even when we need to pay bills. Bitcoins are very good collateral for loans. You can create these either on centralized platforms (and lose privacy) or in many decentralized finance services on smart contract platforms. You can also use Bitcoin futures products provided by many centralized and decentralized exchanges. Since (inverse) futures are settled in Bitcoin and thus such exchanges do not need any access to the fiat world (such as bank payment networks), they often do not require KYC. I recommend inquiring in advance about the reputation of specific exchanges and whether and to what extent they do not require KYC.

Nothing in this text was tax, accounting, legal advice, or recommendations on specific products. Do your own research and consult with experts so you don't get surprised by a bill from the taxman or a hacked smart contract or exchange.

Bonus: The other side of the loan - investing and earning fiat interest

If you don't currently have a need to borrow fiat, you may be intrigued by the fact that you can earn fiat interest - that is, you may be on the other side of this loan. Bitcoin-backed loans have an interesting risk profile in my opinion, where a functional and secure platform can deliver better appreciation than a traditional bank – and with possibly lower risk.

You can be on the other side of the loan – as an investor – for example with Aave or Firefish platforms. With the Aave platform, it's simple - you deposit your stablecoins as if you wanted to use them as collateral, and you don't borrow anything. Stablecoins automatically earn interest. Thus, you complete the whole procedure when you deposit fiat as shown in previous chapters.

Now let's see how it works with the Firefish platform. After signing up, we will select the Firefish Earn option. We choose the parameters of the loan - how much we want to borrow, for how long (we can also choose multiple acceptable options) and the minimum interest we are willing to accept.

Submit your investment interest

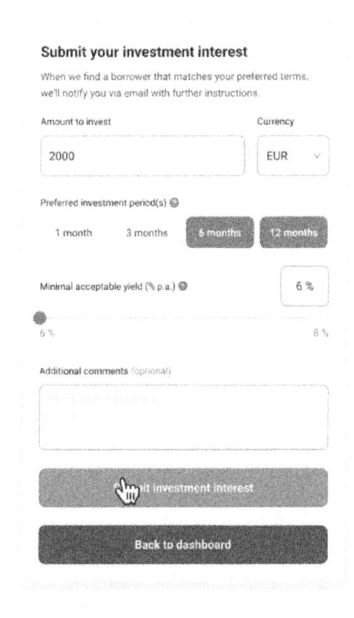

When we find a borrower that matches your preferred terms, we'll notify you via email with further instructions.

Amount to invest	Currency
2000	EUR

Preferred investment period(s)

1 month   3 months   **6 months**   **12 months**

Minimal acceptable yield (% p.a.)   6 %

5 %   8 %

Additional comments (optional)

[Submit investment interest]

[Back to dashboard]

Based on what parameters we choose, sooner or later Firefish will email us that it has a counterparty for us. To proceed, we enter our details, which must match our account - name, address, IBAN and so on. Finally, we still enter a Bitcoin address where we want our Bitcoins to arrive in case of liquidation - if Bitcoin starts falling, or the counterparty defaults on the loan. As with the borrower side, this should be the address of the hardware wallet, as it cannot be changed and we should have access to it for the duration of the loan.

Once the borrower has locked up the collateral as instructed by the Firefish protocol and created the necessary transactions, we receive instructions for the wire transfer:

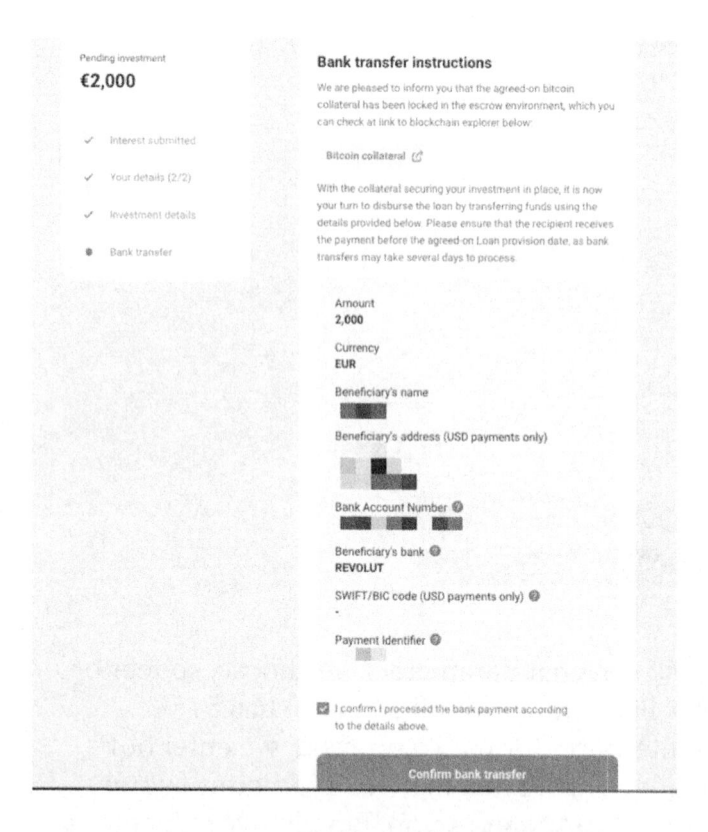

Once the transfer is confirmed based on the given parameters, we just receive a confirmation of receipt of funds by the borrower, and wait for the loan to mature.

Printed in Great Britain
by Amazon